Pocket

KING
CHARLES

Wisdom

Pocket

KING CHARLES

Wisdom

Wise and Inspirational Words from
His Majesty

Hardie Grant

BOOKS

CONTENTS

ON
SOCIETY

'As human beings we suffer from an innate tendency to jump to conclusions; to judge people too quickly and to pronounce them failures or heroes without due consideration of the actual facts and ideals of the period.'

ON SOCIETY

'When the world inevitably
remains in so uncertain a
condition ... the unexpected
tends to occur with
monotonous regularity.'

In a private letter to Prime Minister
John Major, September 1991

9

'I do know just how many
wonderful people there are
doing these remarkable things
and volunteering the whole
time in their communities.
There is something remarkable
in this country about the
volunteering spirit.'

'To get on neighbourly terms with people of other races and countries, you've got to get more familiar with them, know how they live, eat, work, what makes them laugh. And their history.'

'We rush now at such a speed everywhere that life has become so incredibly frenetic, that nobody has time to stop and adjust and think and reflect and recognise that because we're human, and we're not machines, that it is different to being, you know, the kind of sophisticated technology we've created.'

'Human beings are extraordinary
in a sense that unlike the rest
of the animal kingdom, we seem
to be able to bestride so much
of the universe. We have it
all within us. And that ability
to imagine and to rationalise
is totally unique.'

'We don't want to hand on an increasingly dysfunctional world to our grandchildren. I don't want to be confronted by my future grandchild saying, "Why didn't you do something?"'

'History is not simply about the impact past events have on our present experience but about how generations consider, reflect and move on in the shadow, or rather the light, or what has gone before.'

'I happen to be one of those people who believes strongly in the importance of well-tried principles, and of those more familiar things in life, which help to anchor us in the here and now …

ON SOCIETY

... and give meaning and a sense of belonging in a world which can easily become frightening and hostile.'

In a speech at the Newspaper Society Lunch, The Hilton Hotel, London, 4 May 1994

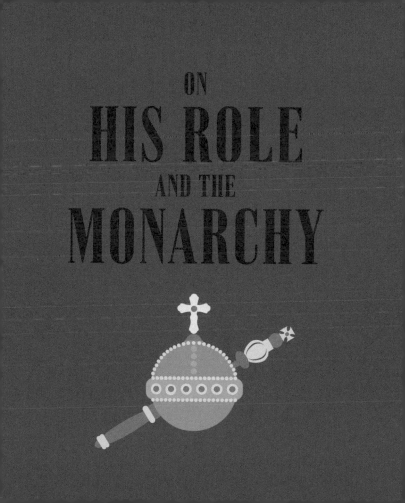

ON
HIS ROLE
AND THE
MONARCHY

'If at some stage in the distant future I was to succeed my mama then obviously I would do my best to fulfil that role ... Sometimes you daydream the sort of things you might do.'

ON HIS ROLE AND THE MONARCHY

'As long as I do not take myself too seriously, I should not be too badly off.'

In a private letter shortly after being formally invested as the Prince of Wales, 11 July 1969

'No, I certainly don't think monarchs should retire and be pensioned off, say at 60, as some professions and businesses stipulate. The nature of being a monarch is different …

… Take Queen Victoria. In her eighties, she was more loved, more revered than she had ever been. In other walks of life, too, age may bring accumulations of respect – and possibly wisdom – which are valuable to society.'

'I find myself born into
this particular position.
I'm determined to make the
most of it, and to do whatever
I can to help. I hope to leave
things behind a little bit better
than I found them.'

'In my particular situation, there
is no actual laid down job or role.
You have to, to a certain extent,
do as you think right.'

'You can't be the same as the sovereign if you're the Prince of Wales or the heir. But the idea somehow that I'm going to go on in exactly the same way if I have to succeed is complete nonsense because the two situations are completely different.'

'Something as curious as the monarchy won't survive unless you take account of people's attitudes. After all, if people don't want it, they won't have it.'

'To be just a presence
would be fatal.'

'Like the monarch, a Prince of Wales has to do what he can by influence, not by power. The influence is in direct ratio to the respect people have for you.'

ON
HIMSELF

ON HIMSELF

'My problem is that I become
carried away by enthusiasm
to try and improve things.'

In a private letter, 3 June 1989

'I'm not very good at being a performing monkey ... I'm not prepared to perform whenever they want me to perform.'

ON HIMSELF

'I always feel that unless I rush about doing things and trying to help furiously, I will not be seen to be relevant and I will be considered a mere playboy.'

In a private letter, 31 March 1987

ON HIMSELF

'I want to raise aspirations and recreate hope from hopelessness and health from deprivation.'

'My problem is I find there are too many things that need doing or battling on behalf of, just the number of things that are under threat all the time as a result of some fashion or other.'

ON HIMSELF

'I have been entirely motivated
by a desperate desire to put the
"Great" back into Great Britain.'

In a private letter 21 January 1993

'I open myself to every kind
of accusation, I'm only too aware
of that. And I don't do it lightly.
I take a deep breath, a very
deep breath.'

'I believe that if people see you
are trying to make a contribution,
they'll give you all the support
they can.'

'I'm one of these people who believes that you need to find the right balance between ... the efficient and the aspects of life that make it worth living.'

'Impatient? Me? What a thing
to suggest. Yes, of course I am.
I'll run out of time soon. I shall
have snuffed it if I'm not careful.'

'I find I have a terrible knotted feeling in the pit of my tummy as the courage is plucked from somewhere inside ...

ON HIMSELF

... Having made the speech,
I then usually have dreadful
second thoughts and feel
I shouldn't have done
it and it would be so much
easier to lead a quiet life!'

In a private letter, 1 May 1989

'I feel like certain things have to be said. If you skirt round the issues, how do we ever get anywhere in life?'

ON HIMSELF

'I want to do something in my life.
I want to start something that will
make a difference.'

'I am one of those people who searches. I'm interested in pursuing the path, if I can find it, through the thicket.'

'If you stick to your guns,
sometimes 35 years later,
whatever it is, you suddenly find
that some of these things are
starting to appeal to people.'

ON THE
ENVIRONMENT
AND
NATURE

'This is a call to revolution. The Earth is under threat. It cannot cope with all that we demand of it. It is losing its balance and we humans are causing this to happen.'

'Since the Industrial
Revolution, human beings have
been upsetting that balance
[of nature], persistently choosing
short-term options and to hell
with the long-term
repercussions.'

Saving the Ozone Layer World Conference,
London, 6 March 1989

'I remember as a child at Sandringham, there was the most wonderful topiary garden Queen Alexandra, my great-great-grandmother, had established at the old dairy building …

… I can still remember
being taken as a child, being
wheeled in my pram even and
it was so special, these clipped
animal shapes, peacocks, birds.
I've never forgotten it. I would
say it had a profound
influence on me.'

'The more we erode the natural world, the more we destroy biodiversity, the more we expose ourselves to this kind of danger.'

'The whole point of gardening
is to give pleasure to other
people, not just me. I see it as an
exhibition. It's rather like painting
my bad watercolours. I just try to
ensure they – and the garden –
are as good as possible.'

'Let's be clear, our planet will survive a high degree of climate change. Planets do survive. But only one planet as far as we know currently has the very precise conditions our species needs to survive …

... And, make no mistake about it, we are well on the way to destroying those conditions, and making our planet uninhabitable.'

May Day Business Summit on Climate Change, London, 1 May 2007

'What on earth is the point
of waiting till we test the world
to destruction, because we
believe really rigidly in empirical,
evidence-based science, before
taking decisive action? On this
occasion it will quite simply
be too late.'

Celtic Nations Business Summit on Climate
Change, Cardiff, 7 November 2007

'We should have been treating the planet as if it were a patient long ago. No self-respecting doctor would ever have let the situation reach this stage before making an intervention.'

'The rainforests, which encircle the world, are our very life-support system – and we are on the verge of switching it off.'

Presidential Lecture, Presidential Palace, Jakarta, 3 November 2008

'The demand for organic food
is growing at a remarkable rate.
Consumers have made it clear
that they want organic produce,
and every sector of the food
chain is responding.'

Soil Association Organic Food Awards,
London, 28 October 1998

'If we could exist independently of nature and her underlying principles, that would be splendid, but we can't – certainly not if we retain a modicum of interest in our children's and grandchildren's future on this threatened planet.'

ON THE ENVIRONMENT AND NATURE

'I believe for what it's worth it
is of crucial importance to work
in harmony with nature, again.
To rediscover how it's necessary
to work with the grain of nature,
as it is with the grain of our
own humanity.'

The Prince's Foundation for the Built Environment
Annual Conference, 3 February 2010

'I don't know what it is, but I'd always felt that there was this interconnectedness in nature long ago. Without it, nothing is sacred anymore and we lose that fundamental understanding of the need for harmony – or balance – with nature.'

'I just come and talk to the plants, really – very important to talk to them, they respond I find.'

ON
FAITH
AND
RELIGION

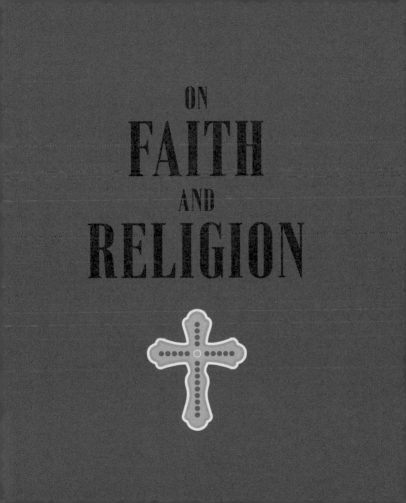

'I mind about the inclusion
of other people's faiths and
their freedom to worship in this
country. And it's always seemed
to me that, while at the same
time being Defender of The Faith,
you can also be protector
of faiths.'

ON FAITH AND RELIGION

'When my heart tells me to
work towards greater tolerance
and understanding, my head tells
me that to translate this into
action we could do worse than
begin by reassessing – calmly and
rationally – our perceptions
of one another.'

Video message at Islam and Muslims in the
World Today conference, Cambridge,
4 June 2007

'Co-existence and understanding
are not just possible, therefore;
they are confirmed by hundreds
of years of shared experience.
Extremism and division are by
no means inevitable.'

At a service to celebrate the contribution
of Christians in the Middle East,
4 December 2018

ON FAITH AND RELIGION

'Forgiveness, as many of
you know far better than I, is not
a passive act, or submission.
Rather, it is an act of supreme
courage; of a refusal to be
defined by the sin against you;
of determination that love will
triumph over hate.'

At a service to celebrate the contribution
of Christians in the Middle East,
4 December 2018

'By working together, we can move mountains. By working in opposition to each other, we simply create bigger mountains and cancel each other out – and worse.'

Video message at Islam and Muslims in the World Today conference, Cambridge, 4 June 2007

ON FAITH AND RELIGION

'Time and again I have been deeply humbled and profoundly moved by the extraordinary grace and capacity for forgiveness that I have seen in those who have suffered so much.'

At a service to celebrate the contribution of Christians in the Middle East, 4 December 2018

ON
HIS FAMILY
AND
RELATIONSHIPS

'We still cannot get over what happened that day. Neither of us can get over the atmosphere; it was electric … It made us both extraordinarily proud to be British.'

On his wedding to Diana, Princess of Wales, three months after the ceremony, 1981

'Relationships with fathers can be such complex ones ... So often, I suppose, one must long to have got on better or to have been able to talk freely about the things that matter deeply but one was too inhibited to discuss.'

In a private letter, 27 September 1987

'Throughout her life, Her Majesty the Queen – my beloved mother – was an inspiration and example to me and to all my family, and we owe her the most heartfelt debt any family can owe to their mother; for her love, affection, guidance, understanding and example.'

In his first speech as king,
9 September 2022

'For me, by far the most moving and meaningful moment came when I put my hands between Mummy's and swore to be her liege man of life and limb and to live and die against all manner of folks – such magnificent medieval, appropriate words, even if they were never adhered to in those old days.'

'He has the good fortune
not to look like me.'

On Prince William's birth, 21 June 1982

'As they get older, the more things perhaps they, being boys, can do with their father. That's obviously more and more enjoyable. But I've always mucked around with them a great deal.'

'All of us gathered here today miss my darling grandmother's vitality, her interest in the lives of others, her unbounded courage and determination that allowed her – incredibly – to continue her official life to the age of very nearly 102 …

... her perceptive wisdom, her calm in the face of all adversities, her steadfast belief in the British people and, above all, her irresistible, irrepressible sense of mischievous humour.'

At the unveiling of the memorial to
Queen Elizabeth The Queen Mother,
London, 24 February 2009

'You have met us and talked with us. You laugh and cry with us and, most importantly, you have been there for us, for these 70 years. You pledged to serve your whole life – you continue to deliver.'

Queen Elizabeth II Platinum Jubilee Party,
4 June 2022

'It's always marvellous
to have somebody who ...
you feel understands and
wants to encourage. Although
she certainly pokes fun if I get
too serious about things.
And all that helps.'

On his wife Camilla, now Queen Consort

'She was quite simply the most magical grandmother you could possibly have, and I was utterly devoted to her.'

In a televised address after the death of his grandmother Queen Elizabeth, the Queen Mother, 2 April 2002

86

ON HIS FAMILY AND RELATIONSHIPS

'How awful incompatibility is,
and how dreadfully destructive
it can be for the players in this
extraordinary drama. It has all the
ingredients of a Greek tragedy ...
I never thought it would end
up like this.'

In a private letter discussing the breakdown of his
first marriage to Diana, Princess of Wales, 1986

ON
YOUTH
AND
EDUCATION

'It seems to me that the problems
we suffer in society as a result
of violence, mugging and general
anti-social behaviour on the part
of younger people, are partly due
to a lack of outlets into which
pent-up energy and frustration
and a desire for adventure can
be properly channelled.'

House of Lords, 1 June 1975

'I felt very strongly that we ought to try and find a way of enabling young people in rather deprived parts of the country to start their own enterprises, because I believe there is a great deal of talent that lies underutilised.'

'Everybody has [a talent] lurking somewhere. It's just they aren't always brought out. If we can develop self-confidence and self-esteem, that's what really gets people going.'

'So many young people feel they don't belong, because they don't have a sense of being useful, of being of service, of contributing.'

Published in 2023 by Hardie Grant Books,
an imprint of Hardie Grant Publishing

Hardie Grant Books (London)
5th & 6th Floors
52–54 Southwark Street
London SE1 1UN

Hardie Grant Books (Melbourne)
Building 1, 658 Church Street
Richmond, Victoria 3121

hardiegrantbooks.com

British Library Cataloguing-in-Publication Data. A catalogue record for this book is available from the British Library.

Pocket King Charles Wisdom
ISBN: 9781784886653

10 9 8 7 6 5 4 3 2 1

Acting Publishing Director: Emma Hopkin
Publishing Director: Kajal Mistry
Commissioning Editor: Kate Burkett
Design and Art Direction: Studio Noel
Production Controller: Martina Georgieva

Colour reproduction by p2d
Printed and bound in China by Leo Paper Products Ltd.

Speeches
www.princeofwales.gov.uk/speeches - pp. 16–17, 51, 56–57, 58, 60, 61, 63, 69, 70, 71, 72, 73, 78, 82–83, 84, 86, 90

Books
Bedell Smith, Sally. 4.4.2017 *Prince Charles: The Passions and Paradoxes of an Improbable Life*. Random House – pp. 15, 41
Brooke, John. 1.1. 1972 *King George III*. McGraw-Hill - pp. 8
Dimbleby, Johnathan. 12.11.1998 *Prince of Wales: A Biography* by Jonathan Dimbleby. Sphere – pp. 20
His Majesty King Charles III. 2.11. 2010 *Harmony*. HarperCollins – pp. 50, 62
Jobson, Robert. 1.11. 2018 *Charles at Seventy – Thoughts, Hopes & Dreams*. John Blake Publishing Ltd. – pp. 34, 77
Mayer, Catherine. 25.8.2022 *Charles: The Heart of a King* by Catherine Mayer. WH Allen – pp. 35, 45

Newspapers and magazines
GQ Magazine, 6 September 2018 – pp. 36
Financial Times, 28 June 2014 - pp. 47
Financial Times, 9 September 2022 – pp. 28
The Observer, 9 June 1974 – pp. 11, 22–23, 29, 39, 93
The Telegraph, 7 June 2019 – pp. 52–53, 55, 64

Broadcast
This Morning, 7 January 2013 – pp. 10, 14
60 Minutes, 15 September 2005 – pp. 12, 13, 24, 40, 92
Charles: The Private Man, the Public Role, ITV, 29 June 1994 – pp. 33, 46, 81
CNN, 13 March 2015 – pp. 85
Prince, Son and Heir, Charles at 70, BBC, 8 November 2018 – pp. 26
Sky News, 5 June 2020 – pp. 54, 59
The Prince and Princess of Wales Talking Personally with Alastair Burnet, October 1985 – pp. 25, 38, 44, 91
The Sunday Hour, BBC Radio 2, February 2015 – pp. 68

Published in 2023 by Hardie Grant Books,
an imprint of Hardie Grant Publishing

Hardie Grant Books (London)
5th & 6th Floors
52–54 Southwark Street
London SE1 1UN

Hardie Grant Books (Melbourne)
Building 1, 658 Church Street
Richmond, Victoria 3121

hardiegrantbooks.com

British Library Cataloguing-in-Publication Data. A catalogue record for this book is
available from the British Library.

Pocket King Charles Wisdom
ISBN: 9781784886653

10 9 8 7 6 5 4 3 2 1

Acting Publishing Director: Emma Hopkin
Publishing Director: Kajal Mistry
Commissioning Editor: Kate Burkett
Design and Art Direction: Studio Noel
Production Controller: Martina Georgieva

Colour reproduction by p2d
Printed and bound in China by Leo Paper Products Ltd.